ALL
IS WELL

DAVID LANGAN

ALL IS WELL

Living Through Losing One You Love

MCP Books
555 Winderley Pl, Suite 225
Maitland, FL 32751
407.339.4217
www.millcitypress.net

Paperback ISBN-13: 978-1-66288-747-5
Dust Jacket ISBN-13: 978-1-66288-748-2
Ebook ISBN-13: 978-1-66288-749-9

"Tears are words that need to be written."

— Paulo Coelho[1]

[1] Paulo Coelho quote, https://paulocoelhoblog.com/2011/08/02/tears/

Preface

This book is compiled of e-mails, texts, and a journal. It is presented as a journal with some of those elements added. It was originally written on the CaringBridge website (www.caringbridge.org) as a way to keep family and friends updated on my wife's health status. The entries give not only a timeline of her condition, but also raw insight into my walk alongside her. The thoughts and emotions I experienced as a committed husband are laid bare on these pages. This is a journey we will all take with someone we love at some point; this book was written to help you find strength and hope for yours.

Introduction

On the morning of Thursday, September 17, 2020, my wife, Zyvonne, and I were in the clinic to hear the final results of a battery of tests from her spinal tap. In March of that year, Zyvonne had begun having numbness in her feet and trembling in her legs, but she chalked it up to competing in many triathlons and seven marathons which were catching up to her.

However, other symptoms emerged through the summer dealing with memory and muscle coordination, so she finally decided to see someone. This led to an MRI, which then led to a lumbar puncture in August. Waiting in the clinic on that fateful day to hear the results, the expectation was for the neurologist to recommend a treatment program or to give a referral to a larger health network system. The final test result confirmed his initial unspoken diagnosis: a very rare brain illness, Creutzfeldt-Jakob disease (CJD), had been causing all of her symptoms. It is a tragic disease with no treatment. The prognosis was that our beloved Zyvonne had less than six months left with us.

In the room where Zyvonne received the neurologist's diagnosis, her calm, considered response was just three words: "All is well."

As we left the clinic, we did not want to simply go home. There needed to be more time together and somewhere else to process this diagnosis. Our daughter would be in her room doing online school (due to COVID). Daniel, Zyvonne's younger brother who had flown in from Albuquerque earlier in the week, would be fixing her lunch soon. We decided to drive to our church and visit our pastor. He was the first person we told. Afterwards, we went through a drive-through and got a sandwich and water to share at a nearby park where we talked and ate at a picnic table near the river. The food helped slow our conversation to find the words that would not come easily. We were not prepared for this when we woke up that morning. We were not prepared for what do to next. After our slow lunch, we held hands and walked down the path along the river, a place where we had biked together and she regularly jogged while training for her events.

We called our son, Dylan, who was in his college dorm room between classes with a few friends. Then we drove home. Zoe was back in her room after lunch in the middle of her last class. We told Daniel the news, and like us, he needed to be alone to process. He wanted to give us space to talk to our daughter, so he went for a walk along the wilderness refuge nearby. After her class was complete, we called our daughter downstairs and told her. Life does not prepare parents to tell their children this kind of thing. At least we had some warning, unlike others who lose a parent suddenly. Is that a bright side?

Then we started making phone calls.

Thursday, September 17

David's Journal Entry

After giving us the diagnosis, the neurologist recommended that we contact hospice to get plugged into their system. He said it's better to be set up early than wait too late when things become difficult. Hospice's service is all about care and comfort, so I decided, why not? Nothing wrong with registering early – kind of like checking in early for a flight to get the seat you want.

Saturday, September 19
David's Journal Entry

The hospice nurse arrived at our house for the first visit to do an initial assessment of Zyvonne's condition. There were several other people we asked to come and help listen with us as the nurse led the conversation. These were people who would help us when the time came. That's pretty much all it was: conversation and paperwork. We got a handbook and a pamphlet to read and also a care directive to fill out.

Sunday, September 20

David's Journal Entry

I took Zyvonne's brother, Daniel, to the airport. He had arrived September 13, and had been with us for a week. What a great help he was to us and very handy: fixing the shed door with our neighbor, Tom, fixing curtain rods and door latches, making breakfast every morning that he was there, and making grocery store runs. Zyvonne's close friend/workout gym partner, Tammy, stayed the several hours I was gone in Minneapolis to drop Daniel off and run some errands.

After I returned home, the hospice nurse came at 3 p.m. to give us a gait belt. This is a wide belt and easy to grasp which helps a person walking with Zyvonne to have a good place to grab if she stumbles and starts to fall. Using this belt is much better than reaching out and accidentally twisting her arm or clawing some skin when she suddenly stumbles.

We had also asked a difficult question about the life expectancy the neurologist gave us. Our nurse, Jetta, told us she doesn't sugarcoat anything, but tells it like it is. That's, of course, what we wanted. Instead of being one to two years, she said that in her assessment, it could be a good six months and maybe up to a year with Zyvonne's strong will and excellent health.

Zyvonne considered this carefully and said, "All is well."

We practiced with the belt in the evening walking up our residential road, but by the time we passed the third house, it was clear she didn't need it right then. She walked fine all the way up and back home again. The week prior to her diagnosis we did a shorter walk, and she said the hill was hard. But today, no sweat. It was a good day.

Tuesday, September 22

David's Journal Entry

A social services worker, Dawn, came to review Zyvonne's information and background. Zyvonne has been a certified flight instructor–instruments (CFII) gold seal instructor pilot, an officer in the Air National Guard, a triathlete, marathon runner, airport manager, a corporate, regional, charter, and private pilot, church elder's wife, and servant of God. What did I miss? What a woman!

The hospice nurse will be visiting once a week, so Dawn will come on the same day, but not as often. We got a larger Health Care Directive pamphlet to fill out for the next visit.

Wednesday, September 23

David's Journal Entry

Zyvonne was her old self today on a phone call from Janan, a dear friend in Germany. She was laughing like she always does with the words coming normally and no pauses in her speech. It was beautiful to hear! That was so uplifting and hopeful and it lasted until late morning when the disease seemed to wake up and take over again slowing her words, hiding them, faltering her steps. This is a horrible disease.

***

September 23

CrossPoint Church Entry
Written by friends on how to support the Langan family

Because we all love Zyvonne and the Langan family, many of you have asked how you can support them and love them through practical acts of service and visits. That is fantastic! We will be updating the "Ways to Help" tab on the website in the weeks ahead with meal train information, various other needs, and setting up good times to visit.

If you have questions or would like to reach out to visit, email careforzee@gmail.com.

You can also leave a comment here for Zyvonne and David to read.

This week and weekend, family will be arriving from out of state and they are really looking forward to their time with them.

Thank you for the many ways you are already loving them through your prayers.

Thursday, September 24

Tammy Lauer Journal Entry
Friend of the family

The Langan family is ready to accept meals. I have connected an app called Meal Train to CaringBridge. You can sign up to deliver meals by visiting the Ways to Help page. You will find suggested foods, time of delivery, and the address there.

Friday, September 25

David's Journal Entry

Yesterday morning, our twenty-one-year-old son, Dylan, drove home from college in Colorado Springs and arrived at 5:30 a.m. Having him with us is so important. He and his twelve-year-old sister, Zoe, have a very close relationship, which we are so grateful for.

I uploaded a couple dozen photos of Zyvonne to the website. I think there's only one photo of her sitting down. She's always so very active!

The hospice nurse arrived at 1 p.m., which will be the routine schedule (once a week on Thursdays). She took Zyvonne's vital signs, which are excellent. They had a good discussion for about half an hour, resulting in two goals: take a walk and take a nap every day. That might sound pretty easy, but for Zyvonne (who runs, bikes, swims, kayaks, skis, etc.), it was hard to take being so limited.

Today, she and Dylan went kayaking mid-morning. Her arm strength is fine, but getting in and out of the kayak was challenging. She was very unbalanced walking up the yard this afternoon. She tried using a single walking stick, but it was not helpful. Next time, we'll try both. It had not started off as a good day, but her dad was scheduled to fly in today from Albuquerque. When he arrived at the house late in the afternoon, she began walking better, talking better, and laughing with him. It was a complete turn to a very good evening. That lasted for a few hours until she said that it felt like her brain shut off and was filled with fog. She went to bed early and, hopefully, will have a long sleep that will not be interrupted by insomnia. Her brain needs rest from all of this stimulation and processing.

***

September 25
CrossPoint Church Journal Entry

From friends of Zyvonne regarding visits to the home:

The hospice nurse recommended limiting visits to just a few days a week. Zyvonne would love to see as many people as she can, but she also needs her rest, time for family, and already has certain scheduled appointments.

To schedule a visit, please email careforzee@gmail.com and someone will be in touch with you. Please do not drop in at this time as there may be something else scheduled or Zyvonne may not be feeling up to visiting.

Thank you so much for understanding!

Saturday, September 26

David's Journal Entry

This morning, we had coffee out on the deck and Zyvonne spent the next several minutes in the backyard tossing the Frisbee to our dog. There were many unsteady moments. Bending down got her off-balance sometimes, but she never fell. Her legs were shaky, but she enjoyed the playtime.

I heard someone in a kayak out on the lake say, "We love you!" I looked up and thought it was the family across the lake, but it soon dawned on me that it was the women's group from church out on an excursion. I think Zyvonne got embarrassed at her wobbliness and came up to sit on the picnic bench with her friend, Sally. Tears started filling her eyes. When I asked why, she said she felt loved. What a great surprise!

Later in the day, it got really hard, then really good, then really, really hard. But the evening is ending well...

***

Circle of Prayer

Tammy's Journal Entry

Unfortunately, it's not likely that all of the Langan friends will get a chance to sit side by side with the family and visit in the next few months.

So, Sunday, September 27 at 11:45 a.m., the friends of the Langan family are encircling their house for a time of prayer. I imagine we'll pray for the family for around ten minutes and wave to the family as the circle goes around the house and family.

Feel free to come as a family and extend your concern, love, well wishes, and prayers.

Please consider biking or carpooling to their home, if possible.

Monday, September 28

David's Journal Entry

Yesterday morning was the first time Zyvonne and our family attended church together in a long time (somewhat due to COVID restrictions). The night before was quite scary because she had a lapse in memory for about three hours. She didn't know who people were at home (father, husband, son, or daughter). It was terrifying for her and us. We were more than grateful when she finally came back to herself. Sunday morning, she was quite herself and very firm that she was attending church in person, regardless of our concerns, so the family arrived late in order to avoid too much stimulation through interaction and activity. The sermon involved expressing love for each other. Many in the church who were able to did just that by arriving later at our home to pray.

When Zyvonne saw her friends coming all around the house, she wanted very strongly to go outside and be in their midst, so she sat in a chair on the back patio as they gathered around her as the central point. The prayers and songs for her were beautiful and she even cut in and said a prayer of thankfulness for them. The family was concerned about over stimulation, but Zyvonne was far from it. She wanted each person afterward to come up and greet her and talk with them.

God gave her the strength she needed that morning, but by the afternoon, she relapsed into memory loss, and this time, it lasted five hours. Gratefully, Sunday evening was peaceful, and everything was restored.

This morning came and we weren't sure how she would wake up. She awoke early (even for her) at 2 a.m. because the normal night sounds which stirred her awake were frightful to her. The only thing that calmed her was reading the Bible. She has been unable to get past any line of text when reading herself; while fluent with each word, she gets lost or stuck trying to find the next line. So, I read to her for hours, following each word and line with my finger.

Much later during a fantastic conversation mid-morning with me, a switch seemed to suddenly flip in her mind and she didn't know who I was or who anybody else was in the house. This lasted almost ten hours. Her body stance at the end of the day was like she had been standing on a ship in rough seas. In the middle of it all, we called the hospice nurse who came right away and helped Zyvonne. She reassured us, but left us with a hard truth: her condition was deteriorating very rapidly. When we recounted Sunday morning to her, the nurse was astonished that Zyvonne was able to attend church and interact with the prayer circle. Truly an amazing gift. She ordered some items for the family (pills and equipment) and left us with a harder truth: Zyvonne's life expectancy is drastically reduced to probably only one more month left with us.

As my mother said to me, this disease is like a combination of the shakiness of Parkinson's, muscle loss of multiple sclerosis, and memory loss of Alzheimer's all rolled into one horrible brain-killing disease.

Wednesday, September 30

David's Journal Entry

Yesterday was a great day, all things considered. Zyvonne woke up today wavering in her mind, but I reminded her what day it was. She had a hair appointment at 8 a.m. and that reminder cut through all the brain fog to be up and ready to go. It had been a long time since her last appointment. When she returned, she was her old self again, which lasted almost all day thanks to the mighty prayers and a woman's love to get her hair done. A photographer who attends our church was waiting at home for her so we could take family photos, dog included. An outdoor picnic on the patio finished off a great afternoon.

I got a call from work putting me on a higher on-call status for the thirtieth (today), but I'm confident I'll be able to stay home. Yesterday evening, Zyvonne seemed to slowly shift away from us. It's not easy to notice when it happens, the transition from friend to stranger, but if she flinches away when I'm close, then I know she's not with me anymore.

Today at about 8:30 a.m., she went to take a shower and was in there for hours. Her saying "ten more minutes" or "five minutes" has no meaning; the bathroom seems to be her safe haven. She thinks everyone in the house is playing games, tricking her into thinking she has this fatal "CJD" disease. Her insomnia has been helped by the lorazepam, which was included in the white bag full of medications hospice ordered to be sent over. This medication makes her drowsy. I had trouble getting the right dosage with the eye dropper the first time; I'm getting better.

Zyvonne's Aunt Michele arrived today from New Mexico. She is Zyvonne's mom's little sister. Zee's eyes lit up when she arrived, and the whole room seemed brighter. Michele will be here for five days. Dylan picked her up from the airport and they had a good conversation together on the drive home. I haven't told Zoe yet, but I scheduled her to talk to a therapist at Stepping Stones next week.

After a wonderful dinner, it was an early night for everyone. It took a while for Zee to actually lie down (it reminds me of my cadet days when we would sometimes fall asleep standing up!), but when she finally did, she quickly fell asleep.

***

The Body in Action

Tammy's Journal Entry

I have witnessed the body of Christ in action over the last week and a half and it is beautiful. Together, you have shared with the Langan family prayers, egg bakes, dinners, lawn mowing, house cleaning, photography, memory books, dock removal, flower bouquets, cards with well wishes, hair styling, massages, and time reading Scripture. Thank you for your willingness to give, share, and care.

Sunday, October 4

David's Journal Entry

Husbands, love your wives... Ephesians 5:25

Writing this journal makes me think I should actually keep a journal.

The two new guests in our house have improved Zyvonne's quality of life quite a bit: they are lorazepam and olanzapine, two drugs that 1) help her relax and stay calm, and 2) help keep her "with us" because it's quite a thing when a wife/ mother/ daughter/ sister/ niece/ friend does not recognize those who love her most dearly on Earth. Some times are much worse than others while others are just unendurable (especially the first time).

Our hospice nurse, Jetta, increased her visits to twice a week. She has an incredibly gracious bedside manner, but I know what visiting more often means. Zyvonne was the one who posed the question herself and asked how much time she has left. Jetta gave the best response. She said not to be concerned with how much time, but to live out each day given. She encouraged us to enjoy daily the things and people we have.

Today, we walked up our street to the top of the hill and back. If my counter is correct, it's around 4,000 steps. She did it with the help of a nice road-walker with handbrakes and a seat, but there was no sitting! It was a high point of the day, yes, but also a heartbreak when I think that that probably would have been the sprinting distance she would kick in at the end of a marathon.

I've often tried to write this journal over the past few days, but the time I set to get to it gets pushed out by many other good things. Soon, another day has gone by and I wonder what really got accomplished. Then I look around and see a mowed lawn, porch handrail, shed door, cleaned house, meals, apples harvested from our tree, a quilt, photographs, flower bouquets, and more. Thank you, everyone. My cup overflows. One thing I finally did was coordinate with the clinic to send Zyvonne's records to the CJD Foundation (again with some help at the clinic, thank you). I've heard the Foundation does excellent things after they confirm the diagnosis and are the nation's specialists focused on this very particular brain disease.

Zyvonne's birthday is coming up soon. I hope it's a good day. Then two days after that it will be Zoe's birthday. I pray, pray, pray she has a good day for that, as well.

Sunday, October 11
David's Journal Entry

It's been a week since I last wrote, but it seems like eons ago.

I've learned in these past days what it means to provide care and comfort to a hospice patient. Zyvonne's head hurts above her left ear? Give her a Tylenol. Her hip hurts when walking? More Tylenol (or ibuprofen). Healing isn't the name of the game; just blot the pain. There is a package of morphine in the medication kit they left with us. I wonder what it takes for that to come out.

Another aspect is quality of life. I've learned that it means keeping a regular dose of medication running through her that dissolves the fog so she can be herself and interact with us in as normal a manner as possible. Otherwise, it's fear and paranoia, hallucinations and suspicion of us as impostors... and *that* is not quality living. She has always resisted taking pills and now is no exception, especially when she's suspicious of us. I have an eyedropper to give one drug in liquid form. The other drug is a little pill I grind to powder and add to a beverage or food every four hours... or else.

Her stability is really wonky at times. It's mostly her legs that will go weak like jelly when she gets up from the bed or a chair. Once up, she can shuffle along and, if really motivated, will quicken to half-steps. However, that usually gets her off-balance and has to be caught from a fall. To sit down, I get her in position and she carefully bends to a controlled fall backwards into the chair. Getting up on her own *will* result in an uncontrolled fall. Last week, I found her on her knees and elbows in front of the recliner with her hands folded like in prayer. I knew she had trouble getting out of the chair by herself, so I asked, "Did you fall?" She sheepishly replied, "Yes," so I joined her on the floor on my knees and elbows. I noticed how much the carpet needed cleaning. We talked. We prayed together. It became the most intimate and honest prayer time we've had in a long time.

Last week, she walked outside and up the road to the top of the hill (those 4,000 steps), and back again. I can't imagine her repeating that now, but she did just that thing the other day with my sister. I think her most recent attempt with our son didn't get her quite as far.

I can tell that she wants her strong will to remain as strong as ever, but I've seen it soften lately. I caught her ire by doing things for her without first asking permission. Her hearing remains excellent, but her vision seems to be fading. Or perhaps it's the processing ability of what she sees is fading. Either way, when it comes to reading the Proverbs chapter of the day (matching the date of the month), she just tells me to read the whole thing. She used to read it all herself, now she just listens.

She slept the longest she ever has earlier last week, about fourteen and a half hours. At the ten-hour point, I was glad she was getting some much needed rest. At the twelve-hour point, I was restless for her to get up. At the fourteen-hour point, my son said even he never slept that long before. We decided to call the nurse if she didn't get up by sixteen hours, but soon enough, she opened her eyes. I had been thinking, hoping, praying that maybe God was using this time to heal her, hoping that she would miraculously wake up and be her normal self, like nothing had ever happened; however, it was soon evident that this was not the case. The disease still reigned in her mortal body. Now, it was my turn for my legs to feel wobbly. I just wanted to collapse on the floor and weep, but I didn't; it was time to return to the normal routine.

Everyday actions we don't think twice about are so difficult for Zyvonne. Things like standing, sitting, going to the bathroom, showering, dressing. Yesterday, I applauded her for putting on her socks and she gave me a sincere "thank you," which kind of made my world close in on me. It made me realize how far this disease had spread and how much she has deteriorated in such short a time.

I received word back from the CJD Foundation that the key test done on her spinal fluid (RT-QuIC test) to conclusively diagnose CJD was, indeed, done on Zyvonne's sample. It's really there. They receive about 5,000 requests a year for this test and only 500 return positive. This opens up the Foundation's resources for Zyvonne to participate in studies, access, and support, but it's mainly a help to the Foundation for their access to her health records, test results, and other material down the road. They want access to her so that this disease can be better understood, treatment trials pursued, causes identified, and so forth. There's still a lot of questions. I have a lot of hard questions, but I'm not asking... I'm not ready for the answers.

October 12

Tuesday, October 13 is Zyvonne's fifty-first birthday. To celebrate Zyvonne, Dave shared with me that Zyvonne wants to walk the Luce Line Trail, a trail she has walked, run, and biked many times. At about 11:25 a.m., she will start walking near Dale's Auto. She will end her walk at Oddfellows Park in the shelter about an hour later. You are welcome to walk with Zyvonne or join in a song and apple cider at the picnic shelter. There is room for about eight cars to park in the DNR parking lot, and Oddfellows Park has parking at the top of the hill.

Tuesday, October 13

David's Journal Entry

Today is Zyvonne's birthday. Last year for her big fiftieth celebration, she organized several friends (with husbands and kids who could make it) to travel to Wisconsin and compete in the Kickapoo Reserve Dam Challenge Triathlon, which consists of kayaking the river, biking the hills, and finishing with a trail run. We all stayed together (over a dozen of us) in a big country home sharing meals, playing games, singing with the piano – very much a warm family atmosphere among everyone. Race day, however, was cold, wet, and rainy. Zyvonne said that on the bike portion, her hands were so cold she could barely move her thumbs to shift gears, but she met her goal at Kickapoo as with every other triathlon and marathon she has competed in, she finished! Her second goal was to always improve her "personal best" time.

Transition to this year's birthday and the gathering grew to about three dozen people who joined her on the Luce Line trail for an unofficial, untimed, half-mile walk. In the year between Kickapoo and the Luce Line, she had continued to run, swim, bike, and kayak, but I don't think she ever competed again. What kept her going were friends who got up in the early hours to exercise with her. She always said that it helped her get out of bed knowing that someone was going to be waiting for her (although she rarely left anyone waiting). Over the summer, her biking lessened because she felt "claustrophobic" if someone got too close to her and she would get unsteady and, eventually, was unable to maintain balance at all on a bicycle. Because of COVID, the pools were closed, so that ruled out swimming except for in the lakes. Her legs were "wobbly" and she had trouble getting in and out of a kayak, but her arms were strong and could keep her going as long and as far as she determined. That was last summer.

Now walking is giving her trouble. The Luce Line Trail walk will probably be the last time she will ever walk any distance. Unassisted, she can't take more than a few faltering steps without falling, so today's walk started with her road-walker. That lasted about fifty yards or so, and then, for the first time, she gladly sat in the wheelchair we had brought along (just in case). As we approached our designated finish near the picnic shelter, she got back to the road-walker and finished the course on her feet.

Thank you, everyone, for making this beautiful autumn day a very special one for Zyvonne and our whole family. She enjoyed sitting on the picnic bench and being with everyone there. Thank you for the many who sat with her, who sang

"Happy Birthday" to her, and honored her. I'm grateful that God kept her mind present with us the whole time. She was so exhausted when we got home that she spent the next five hours on the recliner, dozing now and then, being shown and read the cards, enjoying the beautiful flower bouquets, gifts, videos, and messages. The greatest of the things we have for each other, God tells us, is love. Zyvonne knows fully well that she is loved by all of you.

Thursday, October 15

David's Journal Entry

God answered a couple prayers today, but as usual, his answers weren't how I spelled it out for him.

Our daughter's birthday was a good, good day; that was my first answer to prayer. I now have a teenager in the house again, but this time, a girl! We had a fancy table set with Zyvonne's "candlelight dinner" china and, as usual, a borrowed item (today: a tablecloth). We had about a dozen family members in the house to celebrate. With Zyvonne perched in a beautiful blue blouse given to her by her friends, we enjoyed a wonderful dinner together.

Just two days earlier, Zyvonne had her very good birthday, actually a "minor miracle" as one friend put it. In fact, to be up for the half-mile walk and be surrounded by friends, she rallied in a way that gives me hope for renewed strength. In reality, though, I was told it is a common feature near the end of life. She rallied again in a smaller way today as our daughter was a bright spot to focus on. My struggles and suffering blurred in the background for a time. This disease grows exponentially with each passing day, making each day count as never before.

Earlier in the day, our hospice nurse made a short visit to talk with Zyvonne and did as she promised by not sugar-coating anything. The nurse told me in a gut-wrenching, but gentle way what these rallies meant and how Zyvonne's final days were imminent. Mere days left now.

From years to months to days, and that's all just within the past few weeks. But there's my second answer to my prayer: that God would take away her suffering and deteriorating life. He is a good, good Father, and loves her more than I. I'm grateful he let me and everyone have a way to say goodbye and express their hearts to her. I am amazed and saddened that my love for her has grown exponentially in one month. It should have always been this strong.

Our nurse said that when Zyvonne is moved to Harmony River, the skilled nursing facility in town, I could be with her as just her *husband*. Everything else would be taken care of for her. At first, I felt a sense of relief with that, but as I think of it, by helping her in the bathroom, showering, dressing, eating, walking, reading, I *was* being her husband. What else was I going to do? I certainly didn't want anyone else in my place, not when I was around. When she's at Harmony River, it will be different, but I'll be the same. I'll dote on her all the more and will be glad for people trained to help out, but they will be helping me, not her.

A third prayer that God answered was in terms of support, but he did it in a way that only a real father can. God is a father who sees the need in his child and fills it before the child can even express it. I had signed up to take part in a phone support group with other families going through CJD, but the call was on the evening of the 13th and that was Zyvonne's birthday. I wasn't sure it would work out. Well, it didn't work out at all because I totally blanked the call that whole evening. It wasn't until after Zyvonne went to bed that I realized I missed it. I was wondering what was talked about, so I logged in online. I didn't see anything like a follow-up from the call, but what did catch my eye was a small blurb on my WORLD magazine homepage (https://world.wng.org, and I highly recommend it) about a movie review on the film *Clouds*. Interested, I clicked the link[2] which sent me on a journey for the next hour that lifted my spirits with tears as a fellow traveler — surely as much or more as a phone session would have done.

The movie is a true story about a Minnesota family (from Stillwater) that loses their teenage son to cancer.[3] I started to

---

[2] Clouds Director Puts Lens on Faith, accessed Oct 13, 2020, https://wng.org/roundups/clouds-director-puts-lens-on-faith-1617220740.

[3] Meet Zach Sobiech | My Last Days, accessed Oct 13, 2020, https://www.youtube.com/watch?v=9NjKgV65fpo.

identify with the family (changing the son to a mom, cancer to CJD, etc.). The son, Zach, sounded as bright and shiny as Zyvonne with many friends and thousands of admirers since he wrote a song called "Clouds." This song went viral, he became a little famous, and now has a movie made about his story. Every year, radio station KS95 sponsors a volunteer choir to sing his song at the Mall of America during Christmas at the rotunda.[4] Last year, 5,000 people registered and got t-shirts and sang a great song! Watching their journey in the initial documentaries and reading his mom's CaringBridge entries was cool water to my soul.

While my wife didn't write a hit song, she is just the same sort of person as Zach with as great an influence with others because she had more years to be who she is. I was so refreshed and recharged. The movie is on Disney+ and begins this Friday, October 16. I plan to watch on opening night!

---

[4] 7th Annual KS95's "Clouds Choir" for a Cause 2019, accessed Oct 13, 2020, https://www.youtube.com/watch?v=GW3ZXGjwqVA.

Friday, October 16

David's Journal Entry

When I woke up this morning, I never could have imagined how things would turn out by the end of the day.

Our hospice nurse and our social services worker came at 10 a.m. to tell us the procedures to admit Zyvonne to hospice care at Harmony River.

My insurance didn't cover this, so it would be private pay. Fine.

Due to state regulations on COVID restrictions, visitors would be restricted to just two a day. We are a family of four, but we would work it out somehow.

She would have to get tested for the virus. Okay.

And be isolated (is that like quarantine?) for up to seventy-two hours or more (the upcoming weekend) until the test results came back.

It took me a second or two to digest that, and then the bubbles started boiling. I went ballistic. She might not have more than seventy-two hours, and the state required we be isolated from each other?! I've never felt blood rush to my head in contemptible anger before, but I know what it feels like now.

But calmer heads were with me who God placed there, and through them, he slowly revealed his plan for Zyvonne as they all worked through it. Tammy's parents were snowbirds and their house was vacant for the winter. It had a spacious living room for a hospital bed plus everything that comes with a house. This was graciously offered as a sort of "hospice house" for Zyvonne. Not only that, the many nurses in our church who know and love Zyvonne as their friend were contacted. They all wanted to help in some way, and this was the ideal way. All of them, each one, quickly agreed to help for as long as her time remained. I was amazed at the change in me. I went from spitting fire to being rained on with blessings. The "chief nurse" called me to arrange a timeline. Meal train volunteers would bring dinner to this house for Zyvonne, family, and the nurse on duty. I was just in a daze at the speed all of this was being arranged, but God already had this planned. His people responded to his leading, and a great darkness turned into a comforting light for me.

The hospice crew delivered the hospital bed within an hour. I transferred Zyvonne's personal items, clothes, and the borrowed wheelchair, then my son and I carried her down the outside doorsteps as she left our home for the last time. I looked longingly back to our house and our life, then turned, got into the car, and brought her to this wonderful place. I left shortly afterward to get some other items and somewhere between dropping her off and returning to stay for the rest of the day, I walked into an amazing, transformed place.

Five nurses had already gathered, gone over all the medications, arranged a schedule, and bathed and dressed Zyvonne into her pajamas. I walked into the house as they finished placing her in a recliner. I saw the group of them doing different tasks, moving about like angels. Each one knew what to do, how to do it, and went about it like choreography, gracefully speaking in gentle voices. It seemed like I had stepped into a sacred space. It was beautiful to see how these women, caring for the dying, was done with such dignity and grace.

Thank you, God. It is quite a thing to be part of your family, especially just here on Earth. I hope Zyvonne has more than seventy-two hours with all of us, but I know that the room you have prepared for her in your house will be an indescribable, glorious place.

Sunday, October 18

David's Journal Entry

The decision to move Zyvonne to a private residence has made all the difference. Last Thursday, she had all of the signs of failing fast; Saturday and Sunday, she slowed down to failing not-so-fast. What a good thing. Even so, I said my goodbyes to her. She was engaging in a surprising moment of clarity and emotion with a strong voice and phrasing and said to me, "I don't want to go, I want to stay." I had said similar words to her last Thursday night in an epic moment of emotion, our last night in our home. I also repeated again on Saturday that if she had to go, it was okay, we would be all right. Today, I could tell that she truly understood that. She got restful. I wiped away her tears and they didn't come back like before.

When I was caring for her myself, I didn't think it was hard. It was simply what needed to be done and I did it, mostly all of it, all the time. Now, I sit back and watch the nurses and realize how much work it really was. No wonder I was snapping at the kids and stressing out so easily. I had asked, "Who can take better care of a wife than her husband?" The answer: the Spirit of God working through the hearts of his people. That's a tough group to beat! I was just one person and God was working through me, but now there were these amazing women floating around the room, cycling through every four hours to do their work, their service, and it wasn't hard for them. It was marvelous.

In a marriage where "the two become one flesh," I learned a couple of aspects about that phrase. First, when one is being served by God's people, the other is being served at the same time, too. And second, when one is being taken away from the other, it really hurts. Like a rib being removed with no anesthesia.

A friend was with me and observing the loving service in action toward my wife. "This is what the church is," he said. "It's not a building, it's this...," and he gestured to the people in the room, serving one another. The nurses, the meals, everyone around us. He's right. It reminded me of a previous pastor of mine who told his young son that Jesus is always right there with him. But his son replied, "I need Jesus to be here with skin on!"

Thank you, everyone. Jesus lives in you. You are his hands and feet. Your light shines before others. We see your good deeds and glorify your Father in heaven.

Thursday, October 22

David's Journal Entry

Thursdays are rough days. Last week, there was a turn for the worst. We learned we needed to move Zyvonne out of the house because she was failing fast, so we had had our last night together in our home. Then we got several extra days together with some good moments as she maintained better health. Today, our hospice nurse checked her vital signs and body language and told us that Zyvonne has taken her final turn. Her strong will and determination could not stop this natural process. She is actively dying. If she were ninety years old, it would be within twenty-four hours, but Zyvonne, fifty-one, with a very healthy body and stubbornness, may have, perhaps, a few days, maybe the weekend, she said. It's a natural process that my wife has no control over, so it will take its course. It's an inevitable end, but so hard to know that the process has begun.

The hospice nurse has added the morphine to the drug list for the nurses. Now I know what that's for. Through the medication she's received, she is free from pain, comfortable, and at peace. Zyvonne doesn't open her eyes anymore and barely says a word. "Gotta keep moving," she liked to say... she stopped moving long ago. I find that we want to sustain her life, but are really just monitoring her existence.

The speed of things overwhelms me. I'm so grateful for the tremendous love and support our family has received over the past month in so many areas of our life. I'm thankful for seeing Jesus with skin on, for being a part of His church, for learning how to love someone, for having Zyvonne in my life, and for friends who are really family.

Friday, October 23, early afternoon

David's Journal Entry

We stayed up pretty late last night. I finally went to sleep on the recliner next to Zyvonne's bed after a praise-music song-fest that went on until about 2 a.m. (for me). Zyvonne's friend, Sally (Auntie Sally to the kids), stayed up later than that. It started with Zee's dad playing "Amazing Grace" from his phone at her bedside. Then a suggestion for "It Is Well" came next, so out came the portable speaker. I linked it to my phone with the volume set to a soft and quiet sound. We had been talking and laughing about songs and lyrics sung wrong, and it was a joyful, natural time.

Her dad and brother left, and I wanted to play one of Zyvonne's favorite's: Vince Gill's "Go Rest High On That Mountain." The speaker got moved to an end table and the volume turned up louder. Zyvonne was surely listening with us even though she was motionless. In that moment, I felt that she really knew that we really would be okay, and that our lives could go on with her always in our midst. Sally and I continued to pick song after song of praise and worship with the volume really cranked up worthy of praise music! We sang and sang. I know Zyvonne was joining in because her raspy, clanky breathing quieted and became just soft and heavy. She was with us; maybe until 2 a.m., maybe later, who knows.

This afternoon, I was reflecting on what my pastor's wife told me... how the moment of passing can be a treasured moment as our loved one walks into the gates of splendor, their veil lifted as they see Jesus face-to-face, clearly, knowing Him fully. Zyvonne is hanging on, though. She falls, but then plateaus, willfully, stubbornly hanging on. I spoke words to her that she would say to me, "Gotta keep moving." I told her that she is stuck between this mortal body and her eternal home in an in-between place, just existing and not living, and encouraged her to "keep on moving" toward the place Jesus has prepared for her. "Gotta keep moving." One of Jesus's last words from the cross was, "It is finished." I imagine He is saying that to Zyvonne now, that the good plan God had for her life is finished, her purpose is fulfilled. Keep on moving, we will be all right. And once there, she can help prepare *our* places to be ready for when we get there. I think that thought appeals to her, feeling that she can continue to serve others by helping Jesus get our places ready.

Friday, October 23, evening

David's Journal Entry

> *Blessed are the pure in heart, for they shall see*
> *God.* Matthew 5:8

Zyvonne has passed into glory. She died earlier this evening. She is now in the loving arms of her heavenly Father, seeing Jesus face-to-face!

Through streams of tears, I try to put on a happy face as I write this... I'd like to be real and share her passing with you – I treasure the moment.

I was alone with her by her bedside. The nurse had just left, and I gave Zyvonne a kiss on the forehead asking if she felt cold (just my way of talking to her; I knew she couldn't answer). Her breathing was apnea-style with long pauses between breaths. Kneeling down, I wanted to look into her eyes, but they were still closed. I had thought *maybe* she would have them open just a sliver like she sometimes does, but that afternoon, a nurse told me she was in a coma and completely unresponsive. I had asked her that if I talked to Zyvonne if she could hear me, and the nurse said it was surely possible. Kneeling by her bed, I told Zee that I was going to sing a song for her and sang the first and last verse of "Amazing Grace," one of her favorites.

Afterwards, I took up the Bible and opened it to read the Sermon on the Mount to her. When I got to Matthew 5:8 and read, "Blessed are the pure in heart," I just had to pause and consider how that was so Zyvonne, purely *good* through and through. It continued on with the blessing "for they shall see God" and, again, I had to pause as that was also so true with her. She was going to be seeing God soon... very soon. I looked up and saw a beautiful golden sunset illuminating a gorgeous sky, but with a second look, it was so brilliant it hurt my eyes and I had to look away. I turned to the clock to see the time (5:40 p.m.) and wondered what time official sunset was (a habit from being a pilot).

I was holding one of her hands and she moved the other one up and away, which surprised me because I hadn't seen her move a muscle in a couple of days. It occurred to me that I hadn't heard her take a breath in a while. Did I miss it? I looked at her lying there so... quietly. I started to wonder, but quickly turned back to the page to continue the Beatitude verses. Just a couple more. After reading those, I looked at her again, knowing there had not been any breaths when I had been reading.

I got up to get the monitor the nurses put on her finger to check her pulse and oxygen level. I put it on my finger first to make sure it was working. Then I took her hand again and waited for it to register her finger and light up some numbers... and waited. Sally had briefly entered the room and I called her name. The little screen was still blank. Sally must have heard something in my voice and rushed to kneel at the other side of the bed. I said, "I think Zyvonne passed on." She put her hand on Zyvonne's heart, and then my arm, and said, "You helped her finish her journey. You helped her home!" I knew it was true, that she was gone, but I guess I needed to hear it from someone.

It is finished, Zyvonne. You fought the good fight. You finished the race. You kept the faith. Now, there is a crown of righteousness adorning you.

Looking back at what transpired – with me pausing on verse 8, the bright golden sunlight and glow in the room, then the intense light, her moving her hand – I understand it as the moment of her departure, with Christ appearing to her in radiant glory reaching out and taking her hand, ushering her into eternity.

Zyvonne, I long to be with you and with Christ, which is better by far, but know I must remain and continue here with what God has left for me to do. Many people have been enriched by your life, certainly more than I know. I'm better for having you in my life these past twenty-two years. Thank you for every day of it.

Wednesday, October 28

David's Journal Entry

Zyvonne's funeral arrangements are finalized.

Visitation will be held on Friday, October 30, 2020, from 1 to 3 p.m. at the Dobratz-Hantge Funeral Chapel in Hutchinson with interment following in the Oakland Cemetery in Hutchinson.

Memorial service will be held on Sunday, November 1, 2020 (All Saints' Day!) at 12:30 p.m. at CrossPoint Church in Hutchinson.

Since many of Zyvonne's family in New Mexico won't be able to attend, the memorial service will also be streamed from our church website (https://cphutch.church). Feel free to spread the news to those who otherwise cannot attend.

I've been writing her obituary for a while; Dylan has been helping me touch it up tonight (he's schooling me on English rules and whatnot so I'm glad to know college has been working out for him!). I'll submit it tomorrow.

Zyvonne enjoyed receiving the many bouquets and cards you've sent over the past five weeks. Thank you, I enjoyed them, too. When I considered the main areas of life she enjoyed most, it seemed to center on her faith, her family and friends, and fitness. All of these are combined into a place she loved to attend every year – Trout Lake Camp; the Christian camp our church affiliates with. I asked the funeral director to include, "In lieu of flowers, you may send memorial gifts to the CrossPoint Church Memorial Fund." This is a perpetual fund, a savings account where the interest earned is given to kids to help pay their cost for camp. If you haven't been there yet, I highly recommend it!

Preparing for the funeral is hard, but in a different way than preparing for her death. Having such strong support (thank you!), I only had one thing to do before: be her husband. We never pre-planned anything, so now I'm working with the "making arrangements" part of things. It would have been easier had we pre-planned some of this. In our Dave Ramsey course on financial peace, we learned about having a "legacy drawer" where important papers are stored. We started putting that together, but didn't finish. Then we needed the folder, binder, or drawer for something else, and then the papers got loose or stacked. Now, I'm looking all over for these things. So, yeah, a legacy drawer is a good thing. I'll get that started again with a focus on finishing it.

Thursday, October 29

David's Journal Entry

Tomorrow, Zyvonne will be laid to rest, as they say. I wonder where that phrase came from. Her "final resting place." Euphemisms. The visitation will be in the early afternoon. Our family will have private time at noon and then the published time starts at 1 p.m.

Starting in the hospice house, I spent a lot of time going through a few totes filled with boxes of pictures in plastic folders. We also had oodles of photos taken after 2004 stored digitally. Whether stored in boxes and totes or in files on a hard drive, I hadn't seen many of these photos in ages. The preponderance of pictures were of animals, landscapes, and landmarks, or blurred or dark or just no good. The minority seemed to be good ones of people, but not many were worthy for a frame on the wall or end table. Lesson learned: take more pictures of people and more close-ups. I'm going to bring a few of these framed photographs to the funeral home for Friday and again on Sunday for the memorial service.

Seeing Zyvonne tomorrow will be a nod to her mortality because now, I see her in my mind's eye like the woman in the book *The Great Divorce* by C.S. Lewis (about heaven and hell... not our kind of divorce). The woman in the book was mysteriously advancing in a procession with shining splendor wearing a robe and a crown. The image that Lewis describes is how I see Zyvonne now. If you haven't read the book, let me borrow from a page or two here:

> And only partly do I remember the unbearable beauty of her face.
>
> "Is it? ... is it?" I whispered to my guide.
>
> "Not at all," said he. "It's someone you'll never have heard of. Her name on earth was Sarah Smith and she lived at Golders Green."
>
> "She seems to be ... well, a person of particular importance?"
>
> "Aye. She is one of the great ones. You have heard that fame in this country and fame on Earth are two quite different things."

"And who are these gigantic people ... look! They're like emeralds ... who are dancing and throwing flowers before her?"

"Haven't ye read your Milton? *A thousand liveried angels lackey her*."

"And who are all these young men and women on each side?"

"They are her sons and daughters."

"She must have had a very large family, Sir."

"Every young man or boy that met her became her son—even if it was only the boy that brought the meat to her back door. Every girl that met her was her daughter... In her they became themselves. And now the abundance of life she has in Christ from the Father flows over into them."

I looked at my Teacher in amazement.

"Yes," he said. "It is like when you throw a stone into a pool, and the concentric waves spread out further and further. Who knows where it will end? ... But already there is there is joy enough in the little finger of a great saint such as yonder lady to awaken all the dead things of the universe into life."

While we spoke the Lady was steadily advancing towards us....[5]

It's a grand thing to consider life from Zyvonne's position now and from her perspective. It has been a week since she left this life on Earth, although it seems like an eternity. I wonder what eternity feels like for her with a week gone by?

I will try to emulate the life she lived so well.

---

[5] C. S. Lewis, The Great Divorce (New York: Collier Books, Macmillan Publishing Company, 1946), p. 107, 109.

Friday, October 30
David's Journal Entry

It was a beautiful day for a funeral in the fall. There was not a cloud in the sky and a bit more than a chill in the air, but we were ready for that. Zyvonne showed me how she lived out her faith, being content in every difficult situation, so that's how I started my day, although it got a little intense at times. Every person in our life is a precious gem. I wish I could examine and gaze upon each and every one, to reflect and converse with them on all that they are. I got to do some of that today, but with this mortal life where time is limited, it's impossible to do adequately. Thankfully, there is a way to know a thing without words being said. I wish I had more time for the words.

Many people today expressed how great my family is and that my church is made up of amazing people. I agree. Yes, yes, and yes they are. Everyone served us to the utmost. All that Dylan, Zoe, and I had to do was walk in the door, unencumbered, free from external stresses, and focus on Zyvonne, our extended family, and our many friends.

I've sat now for at least thirty minutes in thought, typing, deleting, weeping, dozing, remembering, typing, deleting, and now listening to my two kids in the next room who are up way too late, but are talking happily and laughing with each other. I won't step in on that. We just buried their mother and there is joy in the house. That's a promise fulfilled!

> *Then shall the young women rejoice in the dance,*
> *and the young men and the old shall be merry.*
> *I will turn their mourning into joy;*
> *I will comfort them, and give them gladness for sorrow.*
> Jeremiah 31:13 (ESV)

Twenty-five years ago a contemporary Christian song came out called 'Beauty for Ashes' (by Crystal Lewis) that resonates with me especially now. It is based on the words from the prophet Isaiah:

> *The Spirit of the Lord God is upon me...*
> *to grant to those who mourn...*
> *a beautiful headdress instead of ashes,*
> *the oil of gladness instead of mourning,*
> *the garment of praise instead of a faint spirit...*
> Isaiah 61:1, 3 (ESV)

If it weren't for God as my heavenly father and the hope I have in Jesus Christ, this world would be all darkness and I would be lost in it.

> *"Who will deliver me from this body of death? Thanks be to God through Jesus Christ our Lord!"* Romans 7:24-25 (ESV)

Sunday, November 1
David's Journal Entry

Wear blue! For the memorial service, I plan to wear blue, which is her color. It was the color she chose for our wedding (royal blue and white), and the bridesmaids dresses were a beautiful blue. Let's celebrate her life together and wear blue. My blue will be an Air Force blue polo shirt, so that's what you'll see me in.

Zyvonne selected only one song to be sung at her funeral which was "Amazing Grace." It was done beautifully at her burial. Since it's the only song she chose, we will sing it again for her at the memorial service. This song was one she also selected for our wedding. It goes way back, is her very favorite, and it is significant for both of us.

Another song she selected for our wedding was "Thank You" by Ray Boltz to thank our families and friends for having such an impact in our lives, shaping who we were. For her memorial, I want to sing back to her from our perspective – as her friends and family thanking her for influencing each one of our lives.

November 1 is All Saints' Day and is a wonderful day to celebrate one of the faithful among us. Let's serve one another with our whole heart like she did until that day comes of His glorious appearing!

Monday, November 2

David's Journal Entry

> *Surely you have granted him unending bless-*
> *ings and made him glad with the joy of your*
> *presence.* Psalm 21:6

The memorial service for Zyvonne was like a prism releasing many colored blessings. Having walked through a valley of intense confusion, grief, numbness, joy, praise, tenderness, sadness, love, hope... the photo montage brought this brief period of suffering and death in good apposition to her zest for life. A huge life filled with friends, family, and activities brought to a screeching halt in five weeks. As the poet Thoreau wrote, she really did "suck the marrow out of life," not wanting to learn that "when I came to die, discover that I had not lived." Zyvonne lived! And she lives on. I see her in the eyes of my children, in the dawn of a sunrise, on the open page of a Bible, in the tune of "Amazing Grace," in a servant's heart... in a million ways.

The song which our pastor sang, "Thank You," brought tears to our eyes again as it did well over twenty-two years ago when she selected it for our wedding. If you know Zyvonne, then you have to know how thankful she is for you, too, and how much you meant to her. I am glad we had it for her memorial because I am so thankful for what she did in me. When I take away my own selfishness and pride, which obscures my view, I see her selflessness and devotion and pure love, new every morning. Some of the quips I often repeat are "hindsight is 20/20" and "you don't know what you've got until it's gone." The memorial really brought with clear vision what a precious jewel Zyvonne is. No doubt she's adorned with five crowns in heaven, and I will be glad to serve with her there like I should have done so for her here. "Husbands, love your wives *just as Christ loved the church and gave himself for her*" (Ephesians. 5:25). That first phrase should be easy; the second is very hard. If we just work on that second part, our whole life will change.

It's quiet in the house now, but the kids are rousing for school (my daughter decided to return in-person). I think the kids and I will work through the book *Heaven* by Randy Alcorn over the next few weeks. The past six weeks are a blur, but I'm glad to have written it down in a place I can return to and honor her. I will always have her in my heart and mind. Now that the caring part of CaringBridge is fulfilled, I'm not sure what more there is to say on this site. It has been good for me to have this venue, to have an outlet available to express what's deep inside and not keep it bottled. It's been therapy for me, and I love the writing.

Thank you, all of the hundreds of friends and family members that are so dear, who have been so much a part of this journey. You are such a part of her life story, how you expressed your love and sympathy with acts of service, cards, and gifts to her, me, and our kids. As her dad said at her memorial, "*Relationship* is more important than so many things in life." Thank you most of all for sharing your life and your relationship with us.

Friday, January 1, 2021

David's Journal Entry

We made it through the holiday season.

Thanksgiving was at my younger sister's home. That was a good departure to celebrate a tradition that had many similarities to years past like the green bean casserole that Zyvonne would always make (this time by me) and enough dissimilarity (like different extended family members attending) to make it a new thing for the kids and I. We felt very comfortable, even though we were the last to arrive and the first to depart.

For Christmas, though, after many iterations of plans on what to do, we finally decided to escape. We got discounted tickets to Orlando and spent a couple days at Universal Studios and the Wizarding World of Harry Potter, and a couple of days at Disneyworld and Epcot Center in all of the villages. There were similarities since we had been to the Harry Potter parks for spring break last March (right before the coronavirus closed down everything) and emotions of Zyvonne being there with us cropped up repeatedly. But it wasn't a sad sort of feeling, it was a fun and even encouraging emotion feeling that she was there with us – her big smile enjoying everything again alongside us, with us. It's not that there haven't been tears along the way; there have been, plenty (even while at Disney, the "Happiest Place on Earth"). Tears spend their time with us and eventually subside, and then a thankfulness replaces the sorrow.

We've learned to think of life from her point of view: the magnificence of the present heaven and how she would so much more long for us to be with her over how much we long for her to be back here with us. The kids and I have been slowly reading the book *Heaven* by Pastor Randy Alcorn. We read it together, each taking a section and passing the book to the next person. We read it for ourselves to know more about what heaven will be like for us, but more so to get a better idea what Zyvonne is experiencing as we really don't know enough about what the Bible teaches on this.

So, the scariest part for our family is behind us, getting through the holiday season without the most crucial member of our family in it. It's also when I realized the truth of the statement, "Happiness is being married to your best friend." I've got friends, some I consider best friends, but Zyvonne as my wife was my true best friend. When it comes to doing anything, it was always her I would consider first in the doing of things, always the first to think of taking to a play, a new restaurant, to tell about something I learned or did or saw or wondered about. That's probably what a best friend is, the first person who comes to mind when you want to share an experience or tell about something or do something. I guess that after I met her in 1995, I never really had any other best friend, just Zyvonne — and then good friends. I can't begin to write how important those good friends have been to me in the past many months. Friends to weep with, to give me their time, their ear, to speak words of healing, give a warm embrace, to listen, just to be present with me.

Here I am, again, focusing on me and not on her. If I think about how her life is transformed, then about how that will be true for us, too, all of a sudden, I'm okay again. You know, there is a tissue box right here by the keyboard and I have gone to it countless times since September as I've been writing this journal, tonight included. In fact, I pulled the last tissue from the box during this paragraph and need to get it replaced because I won't ever stop having these visits with Zyvonne, maybe making a journal entry. The strong emotions are the tie as I see it from the here to there; from me to her. It's how love never ends, always connecting us with each other. I know that things will change, that time heals wounds, that anniversaries and birthdays will be remembered and pictures and mementos of our life will come around time and again.

What remains through all the memories and what ties us all together, is love (1 Corinthians. 13:13).

Afterword

The words of this book comprise probably less than half of what was written on the website. The rest of the story is contained in the heartfelt replies to these posts. So, this afterword is really an acknowledgement, but I felt it was better placed here at the end. Everyone's words of encouragement, sorrow, inspiration, links, Scripture, pain, heartache, love... I read them all. If I responded to one, how could I not respond to all? So, I didn't respond to any.

I want to acknowledge the great comfort and connection your replies gave to me and the kids, all the myriad friends and family who interacted with the words I wrote. There were over 10,000 visits to Zyvonne's story during the four months I was journaling. I'm grateful that modern technology allows such a thing. We all felt close to you and love that you were involved and truly connected with our family.

I treasure the time when your words of encouragement can be transformed into a warm embrace. There is healing in words, but nothing beats having Jesus near you with skin on.

Obituary

*Z*yvonne Devereau Langan was born on October 13, 1969, in Anaheim, California, the daughter of Dan and Deborah (Proctor) Powell. Zyvonne was baptized in her Christian faith as a young adult in Altus, Oklahoma. She graduated from Navajo High School in Friendship, Oklahoma with the class of 1987 and furthered her education at Cameron University in Lawton, Oklahoma with a bachelor's degree in business administration in 1993.

Zyvonne entered military service with the Oklahoma Air National Guard as an airman in 1994. Serving as a command post controller at the Will Rogers Air National Guard Base, she was on duty during the Oklahoma City bombing in 1995. Achieving the rank of first lieutenant, she eventually resigned her commission and received an honorable discharge in 2002.

At age twenty-four, Zyvonne was employed as the airport manager at Altus Municipal Airport at Altus, Oklahoma, the youngest in the USA at the time. She then became a corporate pilot for Shears Construction in Hutchinson, Kansas and later a corporate pilot for Luscombe Aircraft in Altus, Okla. Moving to Texas, she became a commuter pilot for Austin Express in Austin and then a charter pilot for Berry Aviation in San Marcos. On September 11, 2001, she was in the air flying for her charter company when the FAA ordered a national ground stop and she was forced to land in El Paso, Texas.

On July 18, 1998, Zyvonne was united in marriage to David Langan in Altus, Okla. They were blessed with two children, Dylan and Zophia. Zyvonne and David resided in Altus, San Antonio, Texas; Dover, Delaware; Heidelberg, Germany; and Hutchinson, Minnesota. They shared twenty-two years of marriage.

She was a member of CrossPoint Church in Hutchinson serving in the Awana Ministry and many study groups. She was a member of the Civil Air Patrol and the Aircraft Owners and Pilots Association. Zyvonne is honored by a plaque in the International Forest of Friendship in Atchison, Kansas which is a memorial to special men and women involved in aviation. She was nominated by The Ninety-Nines, an international organization of licensed women pilots who recognized her achievements and her encouragement to all who love to fly.

Zyvonne loved to engage in Bible study and athletics. She ran her first marathon in 2009 in Frankfurt, Germany which ultimately led to seven full marathons and several half marathons and triathlons. It's been said that "everybody dies, but not everybody lives." Zyvonne lived! Each day, she rose before sunrise and was always eager to share a morning cup of coffee. Her presence would light up a room as she entered with a radiant smile and a sincere, "How ya' doin?" Zyvonne's relationship with God and growth in Jesus Christ was a daily experience. Blessed be her memory.

Zyvonne passed away on Friday, October 23, 2020, in Hutchinson, Minnesota, at the age of fifty-one years, from the extremely rare and fatal Creutzfeldt-Jakob Disease.

Zyvonne at the flight controls, December 31, 2019.
Image courtesy of Daniel Powell

Author's note: The words in this book have been written from my perspective, but I'd like to end with words from Zyvonne. This is something she prepared for a women's study group. This is her voice, and I'm sure she would love to share it with you.

My Decision Was a Process, Not an Event

God has a plan and it is a good plan

> Jeremiah 29:11-13 (NIV) *"For I know the plans I have for you declares the Lord, plans to prosper you and not to harm you, plans to give you hope and a future. Then you will call upon me and come and pray to me, and I will listen to you. You will seek me and find me when you seek me with all your heart."*

OPENING:

My decision to follow Christ was a process, not an event (Jer. 29:11-13). As I look back and remember my testimony of how God called me to Him, it shows me how He had His hand on me long before. I said "YES" to commit my life to Him from that day forward.

MY LIFE BEFORE CHRIST:

In my early years up through sixth grade, we lived in various places in New Mexico. When I was young, my parents went to non-denominational churches (not regularly, though), so a foundation was laid. My mom had actually been a missionary to a small town of San Ysidro in New Mexico where she met and married my dad. My grandma, on my dad's side, did her best to place a good spiritual foundation for her four children. It wasn't until later that my grandpa came to the Lord.

I remember one time when I was in early grade school at a church we went to, the preacher presented the gospel and afterwards asked if anyone prayed the salvation prayer. And while everyone's eyes were closed, he asked them to look up at him if they had prayed to accept Jesus. I did look at him, but he intentionally did not acknowledge me, probably thinking I was too young. I did not feel then that I had accepted Jesus. But did I?!

We later moved from New Mexico to a small town called Blair in Oklahoma. I went to school there for seventh and eighth grade. I became somewhat popular, but there at that school was an environment that I could have easily gone down an immoral road. God planted the burning desire (can't explain the feeling) to transfer to another small country school in the area, and I did. God, again, had His hand on me. There, God preserved me. This, I believe, was a turning point for me.

By my junior and senior year, my parents fell away from the church and so did I. They were very discontent and angry with God and the church; times had been hard for them. Even though I was not going to church, I knew He was there and He planted in me the sense of right from wrong. My parents were quite morally liberal and surprised with my moral conservatism. In tenth grade, I had, again, felt led to make the decision to stay pure until marriage. God's hand was upon me; this was not taught to me by my parents.

The summer after my junior year at sixteen years old was another turning point for me (God's hand). There was a work program for youth to work for the city in various jobs. I was led to work at the Altus Municipal Airport, where I learned to fly. But more importantly, I was around people who went to church, had good moral character, and encouraged me to dream. God provided me a mentor.

My senior year, one of my closest friends gave me a pretty pink "Precious Moments" Bible for graduation. I thought that it was nice. I had never had a Bible before, but I put that pretty Bible still in a box on my dresser for display purposes. Regardless, the seed was planted (read cover).

After I had worked at the airport a couple years during college, God allowed a bad experience to happen to me to bring me to my knees, to break me, and bring me to Him. I knew who God was and believed Jesus was His Son sent to die for our sins, BUT I was not willing to make a commitment to Him. I had become extremely mean and angry because of my bad experience. It was eating me up from the inside out. I was tendered again. Again, God had His hand on me. He planted people in my life to cultivate the seed. I knew I had to forgive to have peace, but I knew I could not do that on my own (Jer. 29:11-13).

First, He brought a friend named Curtis in my life later that semester. He kept inviting me to church, but "something" would always get in the way. I remember one Sunday morning that he had invited me to church and I had agreed. When he called me that morning to see what time to come pick me up, I told him I wasn't going (I had overslept because of staying out too late). I will always remember his words on the phone, "It's not me who wants you to go, but God." Boy, I knew that was so true; I could not find peace after that. I did go with him that evening to church, but I held on to the pew for dear life. God was calling, and I just would not come! After the service, he shared the Roman Road with me. I sobbed, but still would not commit. I didn't want to commit because I was scared (the Gulf was going on at that time), but because it was the right thing to do. Again, did not answer God's call.

Fortunately, He did not give up on me and sent another friend, Michelle, to be there to answer my questions and, eventually, come up front with me when I finally did say "Yes" to Jesus. It was like a weight had been lifted off my shoulders and peace could finally come. I knew when I said "I DO" to God just like a marriage it was forever. I wanted to make the decision for the right reason, not an emotion. After that night, I did not forgive instantly, but, again, God put people in my path that He used to help me lose the hatred. I could tell I had been saved because my desires had changed. God changed my definition of "fun." Also, through time, my heart was softened and I was able to forgive even though it wasn't my fault.

Well, remember that commitment God had me make in tenth grade to stay pure? God honored that ten-fold by bringing a young Air Force pilot named David Langan to Altus, Oklahoma to me. He had been involuntarily assigned to Altus, he had put in for nineteen other locations, but... God had a plan, and it was a good plan.

Jeremiah 29:11-13